More praise for *In the Land of the Living*

In the Land of the Living is the cry of a modern psalmist. Here is poetry for authentic worship of the wild and unfettered God. This collection should be within easy reach of every pulpit and a companion for those following the Way of Jesus. —**Rose Marie Berger**, Associate Editor and Poetry Editor, Sojourners magazine, and author of *Who Killed Donte Manning? The Myth and Spirit of an American Neighborhood*

Having spent a lifetime at the convergence scripture, faith, ministry, and justice, Sehested brings to voice what he has seen and heard and known in that long, faithful life. Readers will be led beyond themselves in this poetry in the way worship-filled utterance has always led afresh. No doubt good poetry comes from suffering. This poetry exhibits both suffering and the hope that does not give in to it. —**Walter Brueggemann**, author of *Prayers for Privileged People*

This collection is not the standard "plug and play" worship aids. Sehested offers prophetic, mercy-filled, prayerful poetry that demands deep soul-work. Get ready to pray, to sing, to lament, to groan, to shout and to rejoice with authentic, powerful, evocative voices! —**Taylor Burton-Edwards**, Director of Worship Resources, The General Board of Discipleship of The United Methodist Church

Ken Sehested has profound thoughts and an excellent grasp of the English language. He combines them to produce poems that facilitate needed reflection on Scripture. —**Tony Campolo**, author of *Red Letter Christians: A Citizen's Guide to Faith and Politics*

Through Ken Sehested's liturgical poetry, the Spirit is set free to blow afresh. Full of faith and anchored in the realities of our current context, Ken makes the wall between worship and the world a very "thin place." This is a rich treasure. Enjoy, be troubled, be stretched, be transformed. —**Daniel L. Buttry**, author of *Christian Peacemaking* and *InterFaith Heroes*

Ken Sehested has provided us with a wonderful collection that speaks to our human condition. That he has done so in poetic form adds another delightful dimension to this book. There is great hope in these writings. **—Martin Darby**, President, Institute for Servant Leadership

Here is a prophetic poet whose voice cries out against our collective lies and second-hand convictions. It is a gift to have these transforming prayers collected in a single work. I recommend it highly. *In the Land of the Living* casts nourishing bread upon the waters. **—James Douglass**, author of *JFK and the Unspeakable* and *The Nonviolent Coming of God*

Here's the salt for words that have lost their savor. From Psalm and prophecy, ancient liturgy and prayer, *In the Land of the Living* brings fresh meanings to our ears and souls. **—William Johnson Everett**, author of *The Politics of Worship* and *Red Clay, Blood River*

Sentimentality threatens Christian speech. It is with gratitude we receive these litanies. Hopefully these acts of strong conviction will be widely used. **—Stanley Hauerwas**, author of *The Peaceable Kingdom: A Primer in Christian Ethics*

Every age has to retranslate scriptural truth, not just for convenience but in a way that grips the heart with an immediacy that stirred the imagination of those who first heard it. Sehested finds the pulse of a passage and juxtaposes it against the rhythm of our reality. **—Michael Hawn**, author of *Gather into One: Praying and Singing Globally*

Worship leaders will not want to miss this marvelous collection of prayers. They draw deeply from biblical wells and flow freely from the heart of one who walks with God. Every prayer will refresh and renew and awaken. **—E. Glenn Hinson**, author of *A Serious Call to a Contemplative Lifestyle*

Rare is the writer who shines as prophet, pastor, preacher, and poet. With eloquence, Ken Sehested covers all this ground, and then some. He draws his readers into an imaginative dance with both hard-hitting truth and gentle whimsy. This book of litanies is a poignant and powerful invitation to hope. —**Joyce Hollyday**, author of *Clothed with the Sun: Biblical Women, Social Justice and Us.*

Never pray in a room without windows, the Talmud teaches. Ken Sehested prays in a room with wall-to-wall windows, all wide open to the heartbreak of the world. *In the Land of the Living* makes Scripture what it was meant to be: a flash of insight, a bolt of courage, a stretch of imagination, a surprising peek into heart of God. If you want to learn how to pray the Scriptures, start with this book. —**Mary Lou Kownacki**, a Benedictine sister, is the author of *A Monk in the Inner City: the ABCs of a Spiritual Journey*

Rabbis endorse the heartfelt prayers of Christians they know well. Having traveled with Ken to Iraq, when our travel was against the law, in order to protest the inhumanity of sanctions, I came to appreciate and admire the heart behind the hand that wrote of these powerful words. I appreciate the way he wrestles with texts revered by Jews and Christians alike, and that makes me want to stand up and shout: *Amen!* —**Douglas Krantz**, Rabbi, Congregation B'nai Yisrael, Armonk, NY

This anthology of poetic readings, prayers, litanies and settings for hymns challenges our imaginations, prods us from stale readings of familiar scripture, and opens us to innovation. Preachers especially would benefit from this varied collection as they seek exciting and creative worship. Justice-oriented folk like me have longed for a source such as this. —**Wallace Ryan Kuroiwa**, Co-Minister, Justice and Witness Ministries, United Church of Christ

I found myself reading aloud some phrases from this work to my unsuspecting husband because they roll off the lips so gleefully: "Repent and confess you creatures of flesh. Linger and hear, for mercy draws near, bewildering fear in its wake." Thanks, Ken, for a book I'll use often. —**Susan Mark Landis**, Peace and Justice Support Network, Mennonite Church

Those responsible for planning worship services will find this book is full of material that is theologically relevant and rich in poetic verse. —**Howard Moody**, Minister Emeritus, Judson Memorial Church, New York City

For decades Ken has been one of our most passionate faith-rooted organizers for peace and justice. Unlike many, however, his vision and competence extend to the aesthetic and poetic. This volume should be employed alongside prayer-books and hymnals, whether our work is in the seminary, the sanctuary and/or the streets! —**Ched Myers**, author of *Binding the Strong Man*

Only someone with the depth of Ken Sehested's commitment to peace, justice and following Jesus—no matter what the cost—could create the brilliant litanies in this collection. This is the kind of resource progressive churches have longed for! —**Kristy Arnesen Pullen**, The Alban Institute

In the Land of the Living connects heart with words that I wish I had. Ken prays prayers that connect with the God of passion witnessed to by psalmists and prophets—prayers that now we can all pray, because now we have his prayers for our own praying. Get his prayers and make them your own! —**Glen Harold Stassen**, author of *Living the Sermon on the Mount: Practical Hope for Grace and Deliverance*

Land of the Living is a gift to pastors and worship leaders and to any Christian who reads these litanies, prayers and poems for personal reflection. The clarity of his expression wakes up our sleepy encounters with Scripture. These prayers are jumper cables from the pew to the world. —**Maren Tirabassi**, co-author of *Before the Amen: Creative Resources for Worship*

Listen to these and repeat them together. Hear midrashes in a down home accent to make Clarence Jordon smile from beyond. Hear litanies that teach with a gospel wit. Hear prayers from the depths of earth made to make one's heart sigh and groan. Mine does. Hear what the Spirit is saying to the churches. —**Bill Wylie-Kellermann**, author of *Seasons of Faith and Conscience: Explorations in Liturgical Direct Action*

In the Land of the Living

prayers personal and public

Kenneth L. Sehested

All profit from the sale of this book will be donated
to support the theological education work of
the *Fraternidad de Iglesias Bautistas de Cuba,*
a Christian denomination in Cuba.

In the Land of the Living: Prayers Personal and Public
by Kenneth L. Sehested

ISBN 13: 978-0-9767450-3-7
ISBN 10: 0-9767450-3-8

Library of Congress Control Number: 2009930222

First printing, 2009

To order, or for more information, please visit
http://www.prayerandpolitiks.org

Cover design and art ©2009 by Julie Lonneman. You can see more of her fabulous work at *www.julielonneman.blogspot.com.* Portions of the cover art were used within the book, with selections made by the author, who also designed and composed the interior layout.

Publishing Services by Publications Unltd • Raleigh, North Carolina
WWW.PUBLICATIONSUNLTD.COM

Dedication

To the Christian community in Cuba,
some of whose leaders are destined to mentor the
gringo church in how to live without state privilege

Table of Contents

Use this material

All but a few of the prayers that follow were written originally as litanies for my own congregation. In most cases, however, I've removed the repetitive lines that make for good hearing but redundant writing. (The originals, along with other material, are posted on my online journal: *www.prayerandpolitiks.org*. See the back of the book for more information.)

Local congregations are free to use this material as is or in edited form. You need not request permission (though it's always nice to hear of their use). Simply note the source. For everybody else, permission to reprint should be addressed to me via the website mentioned above.

All but a few of these were written expressly in response to particular biblical texts—usually one or more of the lectionary texts for the week. In a few places I have simply paraphrased or adapted the text. More often I've latched on to evocative words, phrases or themes and turned my imagination loose. (Thus the "inspired by" notation at the end of most of these prayers.) Never to supplant the text, of course, but only to allow its dynamism a chance to interpret current realities. Whether done well or poorly is for the reader to discern.

My highest hope is that these offerings will inspire you to write your own prayers for personal and corporate use. I can attest that the weekly composition discipline is itself a potent form of prayer.

—*KLS*

Preface

If required to summarize my deepest conviction in a single sentence, it would be something like this: I believe that God is more taken with the agony of the earth than with the ecstasy of heaven.

From this root grow seven related stems on which the prayers that follow depend for nourishment.

First, redemption is *for* the world, not *from* the world. Among our most pressing needs is a fleshly faith, one that embraces rather than brackets history, to overcome the crippling effect of disembodied spirituality. In the simple but profound complaint of theologian James McClendon: "We do not believe that the God we know will have to do with *things*." Which is why the psalmist's assertion—*I believe that I shall see the goodness of the* LORD *in the land of the living*—is such an integrating factor in my imagination.

Second, vital faith is always personal but never merely private. Saying that faith has a "social dimension" is redundant at best. Forgiveness is not the ultimate consumer acquisition. The grace-imparted soul does not rejoice in itself but in the repairing of relationships, what in the early rabbinic tradition was named *tikkun olam* (repair of the world). As Jesus said, "The one to whom little is forgiven, loves little" (Luke 7:47). Even in the Pauline pastoral letters the prohibition against stealing, and the requirement of honest work, spring not from civic virtue but "so as to have something to share with the needy" (Ephesians 4:28).

Third, doing justice, loving mercy and walking humbly with God are not separate statements but three ways of saying the same thing. Scripture knows nothing of our segregation of material from spiritual realities. The disarming of the heart is intertwined with the disarming of the nations. Long before Karl Marx made the case for economic determination of human choice, Jesus said: "Where your treasure is, there will your heart be also" (Matthew 6:21; Luke 12:34). In Luke's account of the healing of the paralytic (5:17-26), the religious leaders charge Jesus with blasphemy for forgiving sins. To which he replied, "Which is easier, to say, 'Your sins are forgiven you,' or to say, 'Stand up and walk'?"

Fourth, the God of the Bible is most attuned to the places where creation is battered, bruised and broken. The opposite is true for the gods now enthroned. Which is why—for us no less than the ancients—idolatry remains the central problem. Which is also why our doxology—our heavenward gaze, our praise and adoration of God—is implicitly a critique of the ways things are on the earth and puts us at odds with every dominant power. As Karl Barth observed, "To clasp hands in prayer is the beginning of an uprising against the disorder of the world." The flip side of this assertion is that if we are to overhear the Word, we, too, must locate ourselves in sustained and compassionate proximity to those broken places. Being present where the world is falling apart is an essential spiritual discipline long before it becomes a question of ethics.

Fifth, we need a spirituality that will convict and not merely convince. As T.S. Eliot quipped, we know too much but are convinced of too little. And everyone knows that when all is said and done, a lot more things are said than done. The Latin word *credo,* from which we get the English word *creed,* means "I give my heart to." Vital faith is a bet-your-life proposition. Faith is not belief in spite of the evidence, Clarence Jordan wrote. Rather, *faith is life lived in scorn of the consequences.* Theological convictions often raise blisters on your feet and calluses on your hands. Imagine what it would be like if the story of Zacchaeus' confession of faith (Luke 19:8) guided sermons on what it means to be saved.

Sixth, the quest for a more imaginative theological vocabulary pushes me beyond *inclusive* images for God toward *expansive* ones. No doubt, male language for God is predominant in the Bible. All the more interesting, then—and suggestive—that a host of other images, including non-human ones, are present there. The risk of an anthropomorphic boundary on theological speech—whether male or female—is that it installs our hungry little human egos as the point of reference in the unfolding drama of redemption.

Finally, I believe the text is potent. The Bible's passion is not so much to assert its own authority as it is to *retext* the Word made fresh in every age. Reasserting the central role of Scripture for worship and prayer will not result from orthodoxy's protective insistence, of course. It will only happen as ordinary folk, like you and me, find a lively and spirited conversation is to be had there.

Kenneth L. Sehested, Eastertide 2009

I believe
that I shall see
the goodness of the LORD
in the land of the living.

Psalm 27:13

Acclaim the One whose breath is your bounty

Let the room be filled with laud and laughter.
Fill the air with music and merriment,
 with the sound of delight annulling
 the wail of indigence.

Praise your Maker, you wind and wave.
Sun and moon and Bethlehem's star.
 Shout in exultation!

Let all that swim in the sea give thanks;
 all that walk on the land, rejoice;
 all that traverse the open sky, extol.

Bow down, you mighty mountains!
Lift your heads, you humble valleys!
 Roar in applause, you deepest seas!

Oak and ash, black bear and red robin,
 ladybug and dragonfly, you city-folk
 and you farmers, acclaim the One
 whose breath is your bounty,
 whose mercy is your salvation.

Rejoice, rejoice, and again
 I say rejoice.

inspired by Psalm 148

Grace upon grace

In the beginning, all formless and void,
the Breath of Heaven hovered
deep within darkness.

And the Word appeared,
a Word beyond speech, tender, full of grace,
issuing light and life from the Womb of God
to water and stone and all creaturely flesh.

Oh, Breath of Heaven, Word of the Beloved,
Song of Creation and Presence of Peace,
grant grace upon grace to all creaturely flesh.

Oh, Weaver of Days and Rest-giving Nights,
your Word-shaped world has grown deaf
to your voice and blind to your light.

Against every dark threat shine again
the Sun of your righteous radiance.
Let the chorus of angels sound again
your melody of pardon.

Give flesh to your Breath and a face to
your Word. Descend from your Glory
with swaddling appearance to anxious
shepherds and awe-struck Magi.

Oh, Breath of Heaven, Word of the Beloved,
Song of Creation and Presence of Peace,
grant grace upon grace to all creaturely flesh.

inspired by Genesis 1:1 & John 1:1-16

Arise and arouse

The Blessed One is a stronghold of
safety for those crushed by the world.
In every season of trouble,
cling to this promise.

May this Name be upon your lips
in every waking hour.
In every storm of despair,
hold fast to this assurance.

Let your voice resound with praise,
for Creation's Song has yet to be silenced.
In every eruption of brutality,
take refuge in this confidence.

The Faithful One will avenge
every murderous impulse;
the cries of the afflicted
ignite the Heart of Heaven.

When the gates of death are opened, fear not!
The Advocate will never abandon.
Another Way has opened.
A River of Peace shall be unleashed.

Arise and arouse, O Christ,
and roll back the rule of enmity.
Amaze us with your Grace,
so that all shall be well, and
all shall be well, and
all manner of things shall be well.

inspired by Psalm 9

The Name will not be tamed

Every bird in flight,
every creature of sea,
every hair of every head
is numbered and known.

In darkness and in light,
whether happy or sad,
asleep or awake,
there is an Advocate
    who lingers,
    who does not forget,
    who notices every tear and
        cherishes all laughter.

Who is this Advocate,
this gracious Father,
this guardian Mother,
this Presence
    whose Way is peace,
    whose Will is justice,
    whose Weal is shaped in mercy?

This One's Name
    cannot be contained,
    cannot be captured,
    cannot be controlled.

The Name above every name
    will not be tamed,
    will always slip from grasping hands,

will not be hoarded or
harvested for a profit.

The Blessed One comes
to those with empty hands;
to those on bended knee;
to those of generous heart
and gentle tongue.

This is the Master who
abolishes slavery;
the LORD who
banishes privilege;
the Savior who
redeems without revenge.

Be Thou my vision,
O Redeemer of all.
Heart of my own heart,
whatever befall;
still be my vision,
O Servant of all.

Heart religion

AND GOD SAID:
I will give them one heart, and
put a new spirit within them;
I will take the stony heart
out of their flesh and give
them a heart of flesh,
that they may walk in my statutes
and keep my ordinances. *(Ezekiel 11:19-20)*

It is well with those who
deal generously and lend,
who conduct their affairs with justice.

They are not afraid of evil tidings;
their hearts are firm,
trusting in the LORD.
Their hearts are steady,
they will not be afraid. *(Psalm 112:5-9)*

Behold the days are coming,
says the LORD, when I will make a
new covenant with the house of Israel
and the house of Judah.

I will put my law within them,
and I will write it upon their heart. *(Jeremiah 31:31-34)*
For where your treasure is,
there will your heart be also. *(Matthew 6:21)*

Now the company of *those who believed*
were of one heart and soul,
and no one said that any of the things
which they possessed were their own,
but they had everything in common. (Acts 4:32)

Create in me a clean heart, O God:
A heart alight with your passion,
guided by your wisdom,
steeled by your courage and
forged in your mercy!

Elijah and the widow

It is with careless ease that we say,
Bless God, for all life is good,
when the sun shines during our outings,
when no strain threatens our budget.

It's easy, when life is blessed with children
and our ancient ones live long and die in peace.

It takes little faith to acknowledge God's goodness
when terror remains at a distance.

It's easy, when health is secure
and the future holds promise.

But life is not always and everywhere good.
Storms and strains often surround us
and those we love.

Children suffer, loved ones die too young,
health crumbles and terror draws near.

Draw ever nearer, O God of Zarephath,
divine place of Meeting in the midst of
drought and destitution.

Bring us into the presence of widows
whose faith is stronger than famine.

Send Elijah to accompany us to the place
where hope outstrips horror. Provide us
with provisions that neither faint nor fail.

And teach us to say, along the risky journey of faith,
Bless the LORD, O my soul,
and bless God's holy Name.

inspired by 1 Kings 17:8-16

Rizpah's vigil

O promised day
When Joys abound
Unrav'ling sorrow's grief
When vengeance vile
And shameful gaze are
Bound by grace complete

Cast fear aside
O trembling heart
Salvation is at hand
The Word of Peace
Is drawing near: Arise
O Love's Command

O may Your Favor
Be restored, to Creatures
Great and small
Restore to us
The confidence of
Bountiful enthrall

And haste the Day
When righteousness
And peace embrace, caress
When Rizpah's vigil
Bold and brave, heals
All the earth's distress

inspired by 2 Samuel 21:1-14

No fright scars the night

As shadows advance with light's retreat,
prompt wings of the heart to fold in repose.
No fright scars the night, encircled in mercy.

As western sky fades, with compline's approach,
prompt vigilant hands to fold in repose.
No fright scars the night, encircled in mercy.

As silence descends, distraction restrained,
prompt anxious eyes to fold in repose.
No fright scars the night, encircled in mercy.

For Your lap entreats, Your arms enfold,
remind us again of the Promise foretold.
Behold! Behold! The mercy untold!
Our refuge, our strength, secured in Your hold.

inspired by Psalm 131

Linger no more

Incline your ears, Holy Harbor of refuge.
Give shelter for every storm-tossed
and wind-whipped mariner.

The great sea of discontent is
unleashed against your armada of hope.
We await your approach. Linger no more!

Deep is the muck and bitter the mire. Dim
grow my eyes, weary from untended tears
and throats too parched to utter my anguish.

We await your visitation. Linger no more!
Shame creeps across my face as crevices
of despair yawn before me. We await your
presence. Linger no more!

May the scent of our sacrificial songs of zeal
for creation's Holy Habitation, the House of the
Beloved, fill the skies with the fragrance of mercy.

Let the sounds of your steps echo from the ground.
Hasten the news of your uprising favor!
Resurrect in us the impulse of praise!

inspired by Psalm 69

Rouse yourselves

Rouse yourselves, O creatures of clay,
for it is I, the Potter of Heaven,
who commands your attention!

On your feet, O mortal ones! The
One whose Name is whispered in the
wind now summons your presence!

Brace yourselves! For I am sending
you to an impudent and stubborn people.
Speak up, even those whose hearts are deaf.

Cast off your fear, even when you are
encompassed by ascending briars
and assaulting scorpions.

MercyFull ones, do not hide your scandal-ridden
hands or your scorn-scarred hearts. Trust the
promise, claim the power, walk in the light of God.

We tremble, but trust that your grace is sufficient.
¡Alabaré! Praises be!
¡Marchemos! March on!

inspired by Ezekiel 2:1-15

Come again and feed the earth

Enough! says the Insurgent of Heaven.
I've had enough of your bank-bailing politicians
and your private-jetting executives!

Enough of your trickle-down economies
and your holiday-charity binges!

Enough of your bloated-budget militaries
and gated-community developers!

Enough of your water-wasting,
soil-squandering, air-fouling habits!

You who feed on good pasture,
why must you trample every meadow?
You who drink pure water,
why must you muddy the entire stream?

You who are gathered secure,
why must you shove others into dark distress?
You safe-kept citizens,
why must you shut your sanctuary border?

Hear, oh people of provident pasture:
Judgment is coming.
Heaven's Reign and earth's regimes
are destined for collision.

The One who comes will find the lost,
honor the least,
heal the lame and
restore all who languish in anguish.

Come again and feed the earth,
O Master of Rapture
and Mistress of Delight!
Restore your Realm devoid of fright.
No fat; no lean; no shunned or unclean.
Every throttled voice rejoice!

inspired by Ezekiel 34:11-22

Offer your applause

People of Mercy, put your hands together
for the One we adore, lift your cheers
to the Tender of orphans and widows,
to the Protector of migrant farmer and
those crushed with medical debt.

Release your grip on the gods of armed might,
on strategies of shock and awe.
Confound the tortured schemes
of the White House and
raise the burdened hopes
of the poorhouse.

Offer your applause to the cause of the
One yet unknown in the Pentagon and
in the board rooms of privilege.
Their profit margins and preemptive
plans will be confounded, for
the Prince of Peace approaches
with a new agenda for investment.

Rain will absorb every drought and
mercy be restored to the marketplace.
Lush meadows will break through
the developer's asphalt.
Affordable homes will open for all
whose hopes have been foreclosed.

Those who buy and sell the futures
of crops and petroleum, who barter
menial wages for market share,
will confront the One who
crushes the delight for war
and leads the prisoner to prosperity.

> *All praise to the Blessed One whose*
> *name is pronounced in the mending*
> *of creation and in remembrance of the forgotten.*
> *Our applause belongs to this One alone!*

Oh LORD of life, we come to you.
Create in us a clean heart.
Bless us in the work of blessing.
Heal us in the work of healing.
Light our path in the journey of love
through the wilderness of enmity.

inspired by Psalm 68

Great is your faithfulness

There comes a season in every soul
when the Goodness of Creation turns sour.

"God," says the writer of Lamentations,
"is a bear lying in wait for me,
a lion in hiding," preparing to devour.

The day arrives
when flesh wastes away
and bones are broken;
when I am besieged and beset;
when I am walled about and chained.

Who but the Sovereign could bring
such affliction, when my teeth
grind on gravel, when my lips
are pressed into the dust,
when I am made to cower in ashes?

Who but the Maker could
close the Portal of heaven to my prayers?
Am I nothing more than
a mark for Heaven's Archer?

My eyes will flow without ceasing until
the Ruler of Glory looks down and sees.

But this I call to mind, giving rise to hope:
The steadfast love of God never ceases;
the Blessed One's mercies never end.

They are new every morning,
for great is your faithfulness.
Precious are you,
Host of good harvest,
my portion without end.

When human rights are trampled
when justice is denied,
the Righteous One sees!

Listen for the Voice of Assurance:
    Fear not! Fear not! Fear not!
For the Beloved is more taken with the agony
of the earth than with the ecstasy of heaven.

inspired by Lamentations 3

Pound the doors of heaven

O LORD, how long shall I cry for help,
and you will not listen?
Or cry to you, *Violence!*
and you will not save?

We pound the doors of Heaven, shouting,
Listen!
Pay attention!
Are you asleep?

Why do you make me see wrong-doing
and look at trouble?
Destruction and violence are before me;
strife and contention arise.

Pull the alarm!
Sound the alert!
Summon the Almighty!

The law becomes slack
and justice never prevails.
The wicked surround the righteous,
and justice is bartered to the highest bidder.

Are we forgotten?
Cast aside?
Scorned by those of boastful pride?

Then the LORD answered:
Stop your whining!
Pull yourself together.
Your self-pity is embarrassing.

Get yourself a billboard.
Set a neon sign in the sky.
So that even the most harried
soul can see it clearly.
And this is what it should say:

Don't let your fears
get behind the wheel.
Live out of the memory
of God's provision.
Resist the madness
of market forces.

Live by the sturdy Promise,
not the ruptured profit.
A New World is approaching.
If it seems slow,
keep on keeping-on.

Shiver no more; God is not done!

inspired by Habakkuk 1:1-4; 2:1-4

My soul magnifies you

My soul magnifies you, O LORD, and
my spirit rejoices in your Saving Presence.

Everything in me comes alive
when you look in my direction.

No longer will I languish among
the unnamed, the unknown, the unworthy.

Hereafter, for generations, when my
name is spoken, all will know it echoes
the wonder of your Mercy.

Your power is sufficient to baffle the
aims of the arrogant. Imperial might
trembles at the sound of your approach;
but the prison yards and the sweatshops
and the slaughterhouses erupt in jubilation!

With your arrival, the bailout bounty will flow
to the hourly wage-earners; the stock-optioned
executives will apply for food stamps.

In the land of lies and deceit, in the season
of bankrupt promises and boardroom corruption,
the lair of every heir to every privilege
and every power will be confounded
by the herald of your Promise.

Hail Mary, full of grace, the LORD is with thee;
blessed art thou among women,
and blessed is the fruit of thy womb, Jesus.

inspired by Luke 1:46-55

Bounty and abundance

Jump for joy, O people!
For amid screaming commercials
and blithering campaign ads,
the Redeemer has heard our aching voice.

When misery and madness encompassed me,
when anguish threatened to undo me,
when heartache split my soul,
I uttered my cry to any who would hear.

The One who extends Presence into the
most desolate region—even to the place of
utter abandonment—is mighty in mercy,
strong in tenderness, powerful in pardoning.

Be still, restive heart, in the arms of the One
who dries tears, Who swaddles fretful limbs,
Whose light in the night scatters dragons, and
Whose promise is bounty and abundance.

God hears! God knows!
This is our assurance against the ravages of fear.
Therefore we will praise that
Unspeakable Name forever.

inspired by Psalm 116:1-9

In this Law I delight

Happy are those who walk
in the Way of Beauty,
harnessed in the Bridle of Mercy
and according to the Weal of Justice.

In this Law I delight!
May it rule soul
and soil
and society
alike.

From Creation's Promise
to Redemption's Assurance,
may Your Faithful Word leap from our lips
and exclaim with our limbs.

In this Law I delight!
May it rule soul
and soil
and society
alike.

When dust chokes my heart
and fear stays my hand,
I remember Your Ordinance
and am not put to shame.

In this Law I delight!
May it rule soul
and soil
and society
alike.

When highways of ruin
threaten meadows of rapture,
fashion resistance by
Instruction in hope.

In this Law I delight!
May it rule soul
and soil
and society
alike.

To the Reign of Grace, alone, we salute.
To all others we pledge infidelity.

In this Law I delight!
May it rule soul
and soil
and society
alike.

inspired by Psalm 119

Sweet surrender

Oh, Sweet Surrender, inviting our
companionship along the road of righteousness,

Hear the thankful hearts
gathered in this tent of meeting.

You—Honor of the Humble and
Restorer of Faithfulness,

Hear the resolve that
grows from our gratitude:

Pursue integrity, and speak the truth from your
heart, all you who desire the strength of days!

Harness your tongue and guard it
from slanderous speech!

Stand by your word, even if it comes at a price!

Lend without interest and
resist the insult of bribery.

Blessed One, snatch our hearts
from the temple of vengeance.

And plant our feet
on your holy hill of mercy!

inspired by Psalm 15

'Til earth receive her rest

Kyrie, kyrie, eleison
Let mercy magnify
May all my days reflect thy praise
And earth and heav'n reply

Let nothing justify my way
Save grace, unmeasured still
Let every hour reflect thy power
And life with love instill

Two entered in the house of prayer
One anguished, one in pride
Claimed one: *Sufficient is my cause*
I hath no need beside

The other, heart undone, no claim
Could make on vain accord
My breast doth beat, with me entreat
With graciousness, O LORD

Establish, then, thy Reign of Peace
With justice manifest
Unravel all deceit—and shame!—
'Til earth receive her rest

inspired by Luke 18:9-14

Speak peace to the hungered of heart

In seasons of dark desire, eyes strain
for Eden's refrain and flickered light
'mid the fright of earth's travail.

Oh, Beloved. . .

Unleash your Voice of Pardon
from wrath's consuming reign.
Speak peace to the hungered of heart.

Spring from the ground,
hope-soaked, heeding
Glory's approach and
steadfast love's embrace.

Oh, Beloved. . .

Unleash your Voice of Pardon
from wrath's consuming reign.
Speak peace to the hungered of heart.

Let every just and gentle lip pucker
up for the wedded kiss of peace!

Oh, Beloved. . .

Unleash your Voice of Pardon
from wrath's consuming reign.
Speak peace to the hungered of heart.

Goodness is given, and
righteousness granted, to guard
and to guide each wayfaring step.

Oh, Beloved . . .

Unleash your Voice of Pardon
from wrath's consuming reign.
Speak peace to the hungered of heart.

inspired by Psalm 85

Let wisdom's way endure

Listen now, you who linger in wasted lands,
  consumed with wanton hearts:
The Blessed One has eyes and ears opened
and tuned to the cries of your distress.

Give thanks and rejoice, you
  faint-of-limb and sick-of-soul:
An open gate of Quenching Delight
stands eager to receive you.

Listen now, you who languish athirst,
  bowels rumbling in hunger:
Bountiful tables—too wondrous to behold
—are spread as ransom for your ruin.

Give thanks and rejoice, you
  prisoners of misery:
The Counsel of Mercy now argues your case
in the court of the Most High.

Listen now, you
  princes of contempt:
The burdens you lay and the bonds
you impose shall be seized and
shattered and lifted and loosened.

Give thanks and rejoice,
  you storm-tossed pilgrims:
The Stiller of Storms is at your mast,
hushing the wind and calming the waves.

Listen now, you
    barking jackals:
A diligent Voice will sever your tongue
and seal your mouth forever.

Give thanks, you orphan and widow;
    rejoice, you refugee:
Let the least of these join choirs
of angels in grateful harmony!

With Vindication near,
    no one need faint, no one need fear:
Hope and harvest alike abound
from hallowed, fertile ground.
Let Wisdom's Way endure;
        the Promised Reign, secure.

inspired by Psalm 107

Remind us again

As people of faith gather for prayer and praise,
the first act is that of interrogation.

How long, O Beloved,
will you permit envy and
enmity to choke the soil
of our land and souls?

Why are the righteous silenced,
the truth-tellers scorned?

Speak, O Confidence of the Ages.

Train your eyes on
our brittle bones and
hungry hearts. Draw near,
You from whose womb
earth was birthed and
bathed in mercy.

Our land shakes and shatters
under the weight
of its discord;
the sky wails
and the sea churns.

Remind us again,
O maker of peace, O drier
    of tear and calmer of storm,
    that lion and lamb
        share a common destiny.

Remind us again,
    that all is Yours and Love secures.
And now prepare, prepare,
    prepare the Way of the LORD!

inspired by Psalm 82

Annunciation

Hail, O favored one!
But Mary was greatly troubled
at the angel's erupting,
interrupting greeting.

No wonder.
The annunciation of heaven
splitting earth
is always
    troubling
    trembling
    tremulous.
Mountains shake
hearts quiver
at the sound of
God's rousing.

No wonder.
Such announcements stir
dangerous memory:
the crumbling of ambition,
quakes rending high places,
saviors emerging from mangers
to subvert palaces and
princes and priests.

Hail, O favored one!
Heaven's comedy breaks
with a grin: into the womb
of a teenage peasant,

to shepherds standing
in dung-filled fields,
to *goyim*—
refuse of creation—
from distant lands
who decipher God's
signature in the very stars.

With Mary, Herod also shudders,
gripped with fear, at the sound
of this heavenly *Hail!*
His heart, too, is
    troubled
    trembling
    tremulous.
But Herod-hearts
cast slaughtered innocents
in their wake.

Only those with
wombs of welcome
to heaven's Annunciation
can magnify God
and heal the earth.

Inspired by the birth narratives in Matthew and Luke, with special attention to Matthew's unique account (2:16) of the "slaughter of the innocents."

Keeping watch

In that region there were shepherds,
keeping watch over their flock by night.

Keeping watch. In darkest night.
Far from hearth and home,
stumbling on slumbering hill.

Then an angel stood before them, and
the glory of the LORD shone around,
and they were terrified.

As are we, in the face of torturing
headlines and threatening news.

As are we, when our own lives
detour into tangled terrain.

But the angel said,

> *Do not be afraid, for I am bringing*
> *good news of great joy for all people.*

Upon a watchtower I stand, O God,
continually by day and throughout the night.
Then comes the news: the Empire is
imploding, and its gods lie in tatters.

Bring water to the thirsty, meet the fugitive with
bread. In the days to come, the bent bow will relax,
and the drawn sword will find its rest.

Sing, choirs of angels, sing in exultation!

Oh Messenger of Mercy,
draw near to our secret fear
with joyful, triumphant news
of release from our grief.

inspired by Luke 2:8-15 & Lamentations 21:8-9, 14-15

The singing of angels

Sisters and Brothers, bend an ear
to the singing of angels.

Not that of seasonal
carolers who pause at
lace-curtained windows,
offering familiar and favorite
tunes in delicious harmony
and frosted breath; providing
splendid distraction from the
agonized arias of the innocent.

But for angels, who,
in the midst of Caesar's
endless census, erupt
from darkest eclipse
with unnerving news,
startling keepers of every flock,
unsettling every sanction
with the overture of
swaddling-wrapped revolt:

> *Behold the light*
> *for those who dwell*
> *in the shadow of death!*

Those for whom
this *world* is *home*
will take offense
at the herald announcing

this manger marquee.
As with the shepherds,
they will "wonder" at your tale.

But fear not, for these
are glad tidings.
Blend your voices
with the heavenly chorus,
singing glory, and peace,
to God, and for the earth.

Sisters and Brothers,
Rejoice! For
unto us a child. . . .

inspired by Luke 2:8-20

Bewildering Word

When Jesus began his ministry,
Rome was the sole superpower,
governed by Tiberius, adoptive son
    of Caesar Augustus,
whose praises were carved in stone.

From untamed territory a voice resounds:
    Prepare the Way! Unlock the gate!
    Make straight the reach
        of Love renowned.

Caesar was the *redeemer* who brought *salvation*,
establishing *peace and security for the world*,
    the only true *LORD*
        in whom all should have *faith*.

Rise up you valleys! Recline you mountains!
The Word breaks, unleashed,
    from every empire's rule,
        every temple's sway.

Not even Caiaphas, cipher of sanctity
and broker of pardon, can corral
    the bewilding of heaven.

Repent and confess,
    you creatures of flesh.
Linger and hear,
    for mercy draws near,
        bewildering fear in its wake.

Sinew and tear, every sword, every spear,
shall yield to the triumph of Grace.

inspired by Luke 3:1-6

Bright sadness

In the Eastern Orthodox tradition, the season of Lent is described as a "bright sadness."

In the sadness that surrounds us,
our lives, our community, our world,
we give thanks, *nevertheless.*
More is at work than we can see.

Lent is a time for clearing and cleansing.

Dustballs happen.

In the midst of life's crippling failures,
we still give thanks.
In the midst of Fox News' deceptions,
we still give thanks.
Nevertheless, nevertheless.

Lent is a time for checking appetites.
Longings and desires, created for pleasure
in God's bountiful creation,
have come unleashed.

Nevertheless, the bright sound of earth's promise
brings joy to our lips.
Tether us anew to your Provision.

During Lent we follow Jesus into the desert,
grappling with the distorted longings and lusts that
corrupt the world and even our own hearts.

Even so, more is at work than we can see.
The Spirit is not quenched.
How can I keep from singing!

Christ as *Lord*?

And what do we mean when
we speak of the lordship of Christ?
Is this to say that the Holy One
is the ultimate author of
vengeance and retribution?
Of demeaning power and humiliation?

No, a thousand times, *NO!*

The lordship of Christ speaks
of the coming end of all lording,
of the day when the cords of
subjugation will unravel.

Is the Abba of Jesus simply a cruel
human father writ large and limitless?
Does the Power of Heaven
reside in threat against any
who refuse to bend the knee?
Is the Creator, finally, a terrorist?

No, a thousand times, *NO!*

In Christ we gain bold access to that
Power Who pronounced creation *good—*
more than good: delightful!—and Who
has promised it shall be so again.

To this One, and this One alone, do we bow.
To all others who demand our allegiance, we say

No, a thousand times, *NO!*

For this reason we pray that Jesus,
who blazed The Way, may grant you
strength through the persevering
power of the Spirit.

We pray that Christ may dwell
in all our hearts as we are being
rooted and grounded in love.

This is our invocation:
That here in this Circle of Mercy,
and in every corner of creation,
all shall comprehend what is the
breadth and length and height and
depth of Christ's love and, thereby,
gain access to the fullness of
the Beloved's presence.

This is our confidence:
That by the power of the
One at work within us, the
Promise of God shall accomplish
more than our meager minds can imagine,
to all generations, forever and ever.

Amen.

inspired by Ephesians 3:14-21

Come to the waters

The Word of Strong Deliverance is whispered in the ears of all who long for the relief of pardon.

Listen, says the Assuring One,
all of you who thirst for righteousness,
who hunger for justice, come to the waters.
All of you who know you are broke,
who have no way of buying your freedom,
no way of bargaining for joy—
come, buy, eat and rejoice!

Here, in this Circle, the good news is learned:

Come, buy wine and milk
with neither cash nor credit.
Provision is freely offered,
but only to those acquainted
with their penniless condition.

Here, in this Circle, the secret is broadcast to a world built on deception:

Your anxious toil buys bread that does not satisfy.
You languish in illusion.
Lay down the labor that separates
each from the other—and from the Other.
Bare your hearts as
you approach this table of bounty.

We come to confession uneasily.
For we fear that our lives come up short.

We come to confession fretfully.
For we fear a spotlight of shame will shine
on our failed dreams and frail hopes.

We come to confession fearfully.
For the god of Maximum Return
has confused and confounded us.

We denounce this god:
in the Name of the One Without Price;
in the Name of the One Who established
earth's purse and provision available to all.

Having passed through the waters of baptism,
and tested in the desert of deception,
we come confessing and pardoned
to the table of bounty.

It's fiesta time!

Burst forth in song, you mountains.
Clap your hands all you trees of the forest.
For God is not done. Sure deliverance is won!

Isaiah 55 & Acts 4:32-35

Go tell John

The disciples of John came to Jesus saying,
Dude, what's up with this?
John's in prison,
and you're out here
lollygagging in the boondocks!
John wants to know when the
revolution is getting under way.
Are you the Man-in-Charge or not?!

Jesus said to them,
Go tell John what you see and hear.

Go tell John, and Mary, too:
The blind are being hired
as wilderness travel guides.
And the lame have signed up
for ballroom dancing classes.

Go tell John, and Mary, too:
The lepers strut their stuff on
the fashion circuit's hottest runways.
And the deaf are harmonizing
in Carnegie Hall.

Go tell John, and Mary, too:
The dead have kicked off the coffin lid and
put obituary writers out of business.
The poor have food in the pantry
and gas in the car.

Go tell John what you see and hear.
And blessed are all who see
God at work in these things!

All sing:

O, Mary, don't you weep, don't you mourn.
O, Mary, don't you weep, don't you mourn.
Pharaoh's army got drownded,
O Mary don't you weep.

inspired by Matthew 11:1-6

Seasons of crucifixion

We gather in wonder at
the times in which we live.
    As with the disciples of old,
    the seasons of crucifixion seem endless.

Yet life beyond what was imagined
appears and beckons us forward.

Who can believe such news?
Only those with open eyes,
willing hands and supple hearts.

The voice of Jesus speaks anew.
    Follow me!
And we shall follow.

We follow not because of worthy
claim. For our lives are marked by
tattered hopes and failed dreams.

Shame and disappointment
stand in accusation.
But their threats wither in the face of grace.

The voice of Jesus speaks anew:
    Follow me!
And we shall follow.

The humiliating power of the
cross has been scattered; the stone
of the burial tomb rolled away.

Come, my friends. The journey
continues. Provision is promised.
Mercy is assured to fuel the mission at hand.

All with ears to hear, draw near, draw near.
Be of good cheer, be of good cheer!

Loosed for life and love's consent

Following the dramatic response to Peter's sermon on the Day of Pentecost, the text reports that the newly-formed People of the Way devoted themselves to listening and learning, to lingering in each other's presence, to potluck dinners, and to prayer—with praise and pintos, songs and salads, received and given 'round the Bountiful Table.

Hands and hearts, bound together,
loosed for life and Love's consent.
The Promised Pardon freeing
furrowed brow and anxious gaze alike.

Hands and hearts, bound together,
loosed for life and Love's consent.
The Spirit's grip brought all together
and broke the spell of stingy response.

Hands and hearts, bound together,
loosed for life and Love's consent.
Led beside still waters, seated amid
green meadows, fretful hearts and
frail hands revive in pledged allegiance
to the Commonwealth of Creation.

Hands and hearts, bound together,
loosed for life and Love's consent.
Sisters and brothers, this is our marketing
plan—this is our strategy for growth:

Hands and hearts, bound together.
Praise, to God; and peace, for the earth!

inspired by Acts 2:42-47

Greater love hath none than this

Greater love hath none than this:
Than to caress the battered heart
of one whose hopes have collapsed.

Greater love hath none than this:
Than to calm the fears of a child.

Greater love hath none than this:
Than to offer all you can to what you
adore, and withhold your consent from
every imperial demand.

Greater love hath none than this:
Than to honor promises made
and vows professed.

Greater love hath none than this:
Than to hold onto truth
when deceit is more profitable.

Greater love hath none than this:
Than to forestall a vengeful response
to harm's threat.

Greater love hath none than this:
Than to risk everything
for the sake of the Revered.

inspired by John 15:13

I arise today

Wake up, sleepyhead!
Rouse yourselves, all you
who have been sedated
by the mindless blather
coming from statehouse
and church house alike.

Knock some sense
into each other, all you
who have come to believe
that strength comes
from your own hand,
that security is held
by your own harness.

With my own eyes I saw
the Blessed One before me:

> *Christ above me, Christ before me.*
> *Christ behind me, Christ within me.*

Let loose your timid tongue
to declare Mercy's approach
in response to Mary's supplication.
Raise hearts of gladness
for the annulment of enmity.
Let your body's senses relish
the hope of Heaven's embrace.

Christ beneath me, Christ above me:
Christ on my right side, Christ on my left.

For your Lover is faithful, watchful.
God is ever vigilant.
Rare the mother who
abandons her child.
Rarer still the Womb of Heaven
who forgets her offspring.

Christ when I lie down, Christ when I sit down.
Christ when I arise, Christ to shield me.

For you, Most Humble Empress,
guide me in the paths of righteousness;
you disclose the way of justice; and
your Presence makes glad my soul
and makes haste my feet!

From all who wish me ill, afar and anear,
alone and in a multitude, against every cruel
and merciless power that may oppose
my body and soul:
I arise today!

Adapted use of Acts 2:25-28, Psalms 16: 8-11, & The Deer's Cry, an anonymous 8th century poem often attributed to St. Patrick.

Pentecostal passion

Pentecostal power has little to do
with exaggerated religious emotion.
But such power, when granted,
has everything to do with passion,
with conviction. It's not your mind
that you lose—it's your heart, which falls
head-over-heels in love with the vision
of dry bones re-sinewed and aspired to life.

When such power erupts, they
probably will call you crazy.
Have you lost your mind?!
Yes, we will say, because these days
the mind has become acclimated to
a culture of war; has become inured to
the ravages of poverty in a culture of obesity;
has become numb to ecological wreckage.

When Pentecostal power erupts,
all heaven's gonna break loose.
The boundaries will be compromised;
barriers will be broken; and
borders will be breached.
Economies of privilege will be fractured
and the politics of enmity will be impeached.
The revenge of the Beloved is the
reversal of Babel's bequest.

"I will pour out my Spirit," says the LORD:
Poured out not for escape to another world
beyond the sky but here, amid the dust.

Poured out not on
disembodied spirits but
upon all flesh.
It is to the agony of abandonment
that Heaven is aroused.
Queer the One Who fashions
a future for the disfavored.

The groaning of creation is both
an ache and an assurance.
We dare not insulate ourselves
from the one, lest we be deafened
to the other. Birth is at work.
Though the labor is prolonged,
provision is tendered.

Pentecostal power is the wherewithal
by which we wager our lives
on the surety of this promise.

inspired by Ezekiel 34:1-14, Acts 2:17 & Romans 8:22

Only this is sure

Friends, of all the things
we believe or disbelieve,
only this is sure:

We are a delight to the One
who crowns the earth with sky,
who shines on the soil by day
and shelters the heart by night.

Because of this jubilant news,
clothe yourselves with royal attire:
With compassion, kindness, humility,
meekness and patience.

Bearing with one another
in the midst of disagreement,
forgiving one another in
the aftermath of conflict.

Having known forgiveness, by the
One whose breath fills our lungs,
we are granted the power
to forgive others.

And by forgiving others,
we linger in the Shadow of Mercy.
So let us announce the goodness
of God on Mount Mitchell.
And may Town Mountain echo
our joyous songs of praise!

inspired by Colossians 3:12-17

With eyes apprised

With eyes apprised by the urgency of Heaven,
with lungs in harmony; with hands contrite—
no fear, no fright—we raise our humble plea.

> *Christ in your mercy,*
> *enslave every malice,*
> *transform every heartache to glee.*
> *Rain mercy upon us;*
> *Beloved, conform us,*
> *to Heaven's harmony.*

All virtue and valor, bestow on our way. Consign
all contempt to the flame. Be thou my vision—
freed from its prison—with hope confess, proclaim.

> *Christ in your mercy,*
> *enslave every malice,*
> *transform every heartache to glee.*
> *Rain mercy upon us;*
> *Beloved, conform us,*
> *to Heaven's harmony.*

In grace let us linger, content to remember that
life can't be had on the cheap. Extravagant splendor—
lived in surrender—to the bountiful harvest complete.

> *Christ in your mercy,*
> *enslave every malice,*
> *transform every heartache to glee.*
> *Rain mercy upon us;*
> *Beloved, conform us,*
> *to Heaven's harmony.*

Good pleasure

With *good pleasure,* in the beginning,
the Beloved aspired all that now breathes.
Then again, in the Lovely One, even
Christ Jesus, the Wind of Heaven
confounds the wail of rancor.

Come, heaven! Come, earth!
With mercy so tender, adopted
in splendor, all bloodletting malice
shall melt into praise.

Riches of grace are lavishing still,
breathlessly awaiting the fullness of days,
when all will be gathered and richly arrayed.

'Tis now that blood shall serve its purpose:
of fertile womb, and fecund field, the
hallowing hand of *good pleasure's* full yield.

Now redeemed; yea, adopted!
What mystery breaks o'er us.
Every soul, bathed, forgiven;
our inheritance 'fore us.

Good pleasure's remittance from the
Spirit who bore us from fate's crippling
snare to the One who adores us.

Come, heaven! Come, earth!
With mercy so tender, adopted
in splendor, all bloodletting
malice shall melt into praise.

inspired by Ephesians 1:3-14

Bound to this freedom

Happy are you who do not heed
the advice of evil ones, or
take the path of deceivers, or
    sit in the chambers of the haughty.

But our delight is in the Way of Life;
we labor along its path by day and we are
    wrapped in its protection by night.

Because of this, you are like trees planted
by fresh streams of water, yielding your fruit
in season, holding your leaves without fail.
    Your future is assured.

The self-centered are absorbed in empty boasts.
They are driven by foul winds.
They shall be scattered to distant wastelands,
    withering in wanton decay.

The Just-and-Merciful One is a vigilant
companion of all on the Way of justice
and mercy. The corrupt and vengeful
    trudge the path of destruction.

We are bound to this freedom road,
prisoners of this hope, destined for the land
where moaning and weeping are banished,
destined for the land of joyous song,
    of laughter and dancing.

And mercy, sweet mercy. May it be, even for me.

inspired by Psalm 1

Proclaim liberty

Let praise leap from the lungs,
ascend the throat,
rattle the teeth and
flutter the tongue.
The Blessed Haunt of Zion
calls out to all flesh.

To this Embrace, everything
that has breath shall come.
The God who lingers in slave
quarters assails every
Pharaoh's palace:

Let my people go!
Proclaim liberty throughout the land!

Independence from the
Reign of Death has been declared!
The boundaries of transgression
have been breached.

The Liberty Bell of Creation
echoes across the hills and plains.
The God who forges a people
of redemption sets the covenant
of freedom as the bond of bounty:

Proclaim liberty throughout the land!

The very edges of the earth hear
the sound of God's Rousing.
The sun's rising is a gateway
for the Beloved's Voice,
and the evening stars
burst into freedom song.

The God who waters the earth
and sprouts Abundant harvest,
who clothes the meadow and silences
the roaring sea, makes this demand
of every citizen of Mercy:

Proclaim liberty throughout the land!

Let no one lift a coin of gold and say:
In God We Trust.
The shekel's rule and the shackle's
restraint shall feel the wrath of the
One who sets prisoners free. In this
confidence, sing and shout together,
lift every voice and sing:

Proclaim liberty throughout the land!

Labor Day

Creator God, we give thanks this day for work:
for work that sustains; for work that fulfills;
for work which, however tiring, also satisfies
and resonates with Your labor in creation.

As part of our thanks we intercede
for those who have no work,
who have too much or too little work;
who work at jobs that demean or destroy,
work that profits the few
at the expense of the many.

Blessed One, extend your redemptive purpose
in the many and varied places of our work.
In factory or field, in sheltered office
or under open sky, using technical knowledge
or physical strength, working with machines
or with people or with the earth itself.

Together we promise:
To bring the full weight of our intelligence
and strength to our work.

Together we promise:
To make our place of work a place of safety
and respect for all with whom we labor.

Together we refuse:
To engage in work that harms another,
that promotes injustice or violence,
that damages the earth or otherwise
betrays the common good;
or to resign ourselves to economic

arrangements that widen the gap
between rich and poor.

Together we refuse:
To allow our work to infringe
on time with our families and friends,
with our community of faith,
with the rhythm of Sabbath rest.

Together we affirm:
The rights of all to work that both
fulfills and sustains: to just wages
and to contentment.

Together we affirm:
That the redeeming and transforming
power of the Gospel, with all its
demands for justice and its promises
of mercy, is as relevant to the workplace
as to the sanctuaries of faith and family.

We make these *promises,*
we speak these *refusals*
and we offer these *affirmations*
as offerings to You, O God—
who labors with purpose and
lingers in laughter—in response
to your ever-present grace, as
symbols of our ongoing repentance
and transformation, and in hope
that one day all the world
shall eat and be satisfied.
Amen.

Prosper the work of every generous hand

The earth and all its environs were
marked from the beginning
as the Dwelling Place of abundance.
In this once-and-future land
the arrogant are humbled by
the countenance of Truth.

Holy the Name,
whose might
is manifest in mercy.
Prosper the work of
every generous hand.

Turn back, O merchants of misery.
Your market rule shall wither
in the Light of Heaven's approach.

Holy the Name,
whose majesty is
forged in meekness.
Prosper the work of
every generous hand.

The Author of Eden lays claim
to creation's purpose, raging
against the banker's deceit,
overwhelming the financier's fraud,
sweeping away the march of
capital that siphons the poor
to the engine of greed.

Holy the Name,
whose dominion
frustrates every
pharaoh's reign.
Prosper the work of
every generous hand.

O Troubler of every tyranny, inspire
again the bountiful harvest beyond
the speculator's reach and
the broker's control.
May the quarrel of your love
reverse the rule of theft and
restore an economy of grace.

Holy the Name,
whose blessing is bestowed
on every hungry heart—
and who prospers the work
of every generous hand.

inspired by Psalm 90

Don't go cheap

Sisters and brothers, heed the appeal
of Heaven's approach: The sinews
of life grow from bodies adorned
with the countenance of mercy.

Conform no more to the ruling
arrangements. Don't go cheap
for the marketer's bribe.

Let the eyes of your soul be refocused.
Let the ears of your heart be retuned.
Hold onto your birthright.
Hold out for more:
Don't go cheap for pleasant lies.

Sort the news. Weigh the claims.
Hawkers abound, shilling for those
invested in the way things are.
Hold out for more:
Don't go cheap for second-hand convictions.

If one of you has a special ability, what of it?
Don't be vain. It is not for you.
Fear of its loss will poison your well.
Hold out for more:
Don't go cheap for flattery's promise.

If one of you says, "I have no gifts to give,"
again I say, "Don't be vain."

Fear of its lack will poison your well.
Hold out for more:
Don't go cheap for scarcity's threat.

I, the Guarantor of the Harvest,
have dug many wells in your terrain.
They flow from one to the other
in ways you cannot comprehend.
And all draw from the same
aquifer of life, freely given.
Hold out for more:
Don't go cheap for private access.

inspired by Romans 12:1-8

Shower encouragement everywhere you go

Revel in the Beloved's presence,
every day and every way.
Organize every nerve in
your body to help you stay
in touch with God's nearness.

Fretfulness and anxiety are
like monsters in the closet.
Get up, go over and
throw open the door, yelling
  AM-SCRAY! Get lost!

Trust the deepest longings
of your heart with the One
who takes great delight
in loving you. Make
gratitude your point of
orientation every day,
and do everything you
can to stay on its trail.

If you practice these things,
your life will experience the kind
of buoyancy that will keep you afloat
even in the worst storm. Indeed,
the greatest peace possible is
the fearless confidence
that nothing essential
can be taken from you.

In the grip of Serenity's Presence
you'll be able to think clearly
in the midst of turmoil; and
your heart will guide you,
even in the worst wilderness,
to the place of refuge and nourishment.
Shower encouragement everywhere you go.

inspired by Philippians 4:4-7

Bread-baking God

Bread-baking,
kitchen-dwelling,
breast-feeding God,
hungry and thirsty
we return to your lap
and to your table again.

Fill us again
with the bread that satisfies,
with milk that nourishes.
Drench parched throats
with wet wonder.
Feed us til
we want no more.

We come to your lap
and to your table
and rediscover your romance
with the world.
Feed us 'til
we want no more.

As you nourish us
with the bread of life
and the milk of your Word,
let your Spirit hang an apron
around our necks,
fashioned and patterned
like that worn by our
LORD-become-friend, Jesus.

Instruct us,
here in the halls
of your kitchen-kingdom,
with the recipes of mercy
and forgiveness,
of compassion and redemption.

Leaven our lives
'til they rise in praise:
Offered, blessed and broken
for the healing of the nations.

Heaven's delight and earth's repose

Worthy, worthy the One who
conceived the earth and gave birth
to bears and basil and beatitudes alike.

We extol you, Heaven's Delight
and Earth's Repose!

O children of Christ's embrace, even
when trembling abounds, say aloud:
God is worth the trouble!

The Beloved is abundantly good,
overflowing with mercy,
glacially slow to anger,
drawing near to every listening ear.

So now, every hill and habitation,
every honeybee and human heart,
rejoice and give thanks. For the
Consort of Mary stands ready,
eager to satisfy every creaturely desire.

Worthy, worthy the One that
inspires compassion,
Who disarms the heart and
confuses the tongues of empire.

We listen for that Voice!

inspired by Psalm 145

Hallelujah

The Lord's my shepherd, I'll not want
Green pastures rise and from the font
Flow waters, ever gentle, to surround me
My soul restored, my heart aflame
My feet will walk and for that Name
My lungs will lift to sing, Hallelujah!

Chorus
Hallelujah • Hallelujah • Hallelujah • Hallelujah

In darkest valley, I'll not fear
Though evil threat be crouching near
Your Presence ever shadows and enfolds me
At banquet feast you bid me rest
With enemies as table guests
My cup o'erflows with shouts of Hallelujah!
Chorus

Now goodness rests upon my head
To follow all my days, no dread
But mercy comes running to embrace me
With love's refrain I shall obtain
A dwelling place in God's new Reign
And fallow fields in chorus yield hallelujah!
Chorus

inspired by Leondard Cohen's song by the same title and Psalm 23

Satisfy the earth

In the beginning the Verdant One
saw everything that was made, and behold,
it was lavish and delightful. *(Genesis 1:31)*

The earth is satisfied with
the fruit of God's greening hand. *(Psalm 104:13)*

Let the heavens be glad
and the earth applaud.
Let the sea roar, and the field exult,
and all trees of the forest rejoice. *(Psalm 96:11-12)*

For the earth is the Lord's
and the fullness thereof. *(Psalm 24:1)*

Give thanks, sun and moon;
praise God, shining stars!
Fire and hail, snow and frost,
stormy wind fulfilling God's command!
Mountains and hills, fruit trees and cedars!
Beasts and cattle, creeping things and flying birds!
Let all praise the name of your Maker. *(Psalm 148:3, 7-10, 13)*

The heavens are telling
the glory of God. *(Psalm 19:1)*

Why then is there no faithfulness or mercy,
no knowledge of God? Lo, the envoys of
peace weep bitterly and the land mourns.
From every house framed in greed,
the stone cries out from the wall and
the beam from the woodwork responds.

(Hosea 4:1, 3; Isaiah 33:7, 9, 10; Habakkuk 2:9-11)

If you defile the land,
it will vomit you out. *(Leviticus 18:28)*

Nevertheless, the days are coming,
says the Beloved, when the mountains
shall drip sweet wine. On that day
I will make a covenant with the
beasts of the field, the birds of the air,
and the creeping things of the ground;
and I will abolish the bow, the sword,
and war from the land, and make you
lie down in safety. *(Amos 9:13; Hosea 2:18)*

You will go out in joy and be led forth in peace;
the mountains and the hills will burst into song,
and all the trees will clap their hands. *(Isaiah 55:12)*

Ask the animals,
and they will instruct you;
the birds of the air,
and they will tell you;
ask the plants of the earth,
and they will teach you;
and the fish of the sea
will declare to you.
In God's hand is the life of
every living thing. *(Job 12:7-8, 10)*

Give applause and acclaim
to the bounteous Name
who grants beauty its
grandeur and fame!

Send me

It was a time of great turmoil in the land.
The Spirit of God bypassed all the famous
leaders and came to me with a dream.

And I saw the Ruler of All Creation
    sitting on a throne, high and lofty,
with majesty filling the sky
    as far as the eye could see.

Angels filled the air, shouting,
    Holy, holy, holy!
    Just and Righteous
        and Merciful is God's name!
    Every bit of the earth is
        filled with the Blessed One's caress!

And in my vision, Heaven's Voice made the mountains
shake and the meadows rumble.

And I said,
    I am not worthy to see such things!
        My lips cannot speak such wonder.
            My hands cannot hold it.
                I am only a little girl.

But the One who breathes every breath
    said to me:
        Do not say "I am only a little girl."
            For you shall go where I send you,
                speak what I command you.
                Fear not, fear not.

That's when the Hand of Strength
reached out and touched my mouth,
        saying,
            I am putting my words in your mouth.

It was as if coals of fire reached my lips.
Not with pain, but with cleansing speech
        and clarifying conviction.

And I said:
        OK. Here I am.
            Send me where you want me to go.

Blessed is the journey
        in and through the turmoil.
And blessed is the One who
        seeks the abandoned, who
sings the harmony of life,
        who sows the seeds of justice
and reaps the harvest of peace.

Send us. Send me.
So let it be.
Amen and Amen.

inspired by Isaiah 6:1-8 & Jeremiah 1:7-9

Hosanna's home in flesh and blood

In Joppa and Jerusalem,
in Atlanta and Asheville,
people of prayer are prone
to catching a glimpse
of Heaven's Bidding.

The ecstatic vision rises up
in the midst of pots and pans,
unswept floors, workday
boredom and endless *to-do* lists.
The ancient witness speaks like this:

> *Then I saw a new heaven*
> *and a new earth, for*
> *all that had come before*
> *was renewed and redeemed.*

And I saw a holy habitation,
big cities and small burgs,
meadows and mountains,
all shedding their enmity
in response to God's rhapsody,
each as a lover anticipating the Beloved.

> *Make way, make way, for all excluded*
> *are destined for embrace.*

Look and see!
Hosanna's Home breaks out in flesh
and blood, claiming river and raven,
harvest and heretic.

Look and see!
Amazing grace erupts
in every tear gland
and funeral parlor,
in every orphanage and
operating room.

Death's dominion shall end,
every terror shall bend,
to the sound of
grace unrestrained.

Look and see! Let it be, let it be!
May it be so today, with you
and with me.

inspired by Revelation 21:1-4

For what do we hope?

For what do we hope?

We hope for the Beloved's Promise to
 overtake the world's broken-hearted threat.

For what do we long?

We long for the moist goodness of God
 to outlast the parched climate of despair.

For what do we lack?

We lack for nothing—
 save the need for hearts enlarged by the
 assurance that every hostage will be freed.

For what do we strive?

We strive for lives marked by goodness,
 purified of deceit and malice, and
 hands made gentle by the tender caress
 of Wisdom's approach.

For what do we struggle?

We struggle for the fate of every child
 whose sighs and cries are muffled
 by the market's disdain.

In what do we rejoice?

We rejoice in rebellious acts of abundance
in the face of every stingy arrangement.

For what prize do our eyes arise?

Our eyes arise for the Beloved Community's
embrace of earth's abode and Heaven's favor.

As-salaam alaykum.
Peace be with you!
Wa alaykum as-salaam.
And with you, peace!

Benedicere

May your home always be too
small to hold all your friends.

May your heart remain ever supple,
fearless in the face of threat,
jubilant in the grip of grace.

May your hands remain open,
caressing, never clenched,
save to pound the doors of all who
barter justice to the highest bidder.

May your heroes be earthy,
dusty-shoed and rumpled,
hallowed but unhaloed,
guiding you through seasons
of tremor and travail, apprenticed
to the godly art of giggling amid
haggard news and portentous circumstance.

May your hankering be
in rhythm with heaven's,
whose covenant vows a dusty
intersection with our own:
when creation's hope and history rhyme.

May hosannas lilt from your lungs:
God is not done;
God is not yet done.

All flesh, I am told, will behold;
will surely behold.

Endnotes

Arise and arouse. A shorter version of this prayer appears in *Before the Amen: Creative Resources for Worship*, Maren C. Tirabasi & Maria I. Tirabassi, eds., Pilgrim Press 2007. The last line comes from Julian of Norwich, a 14th century mystic.

Benedicere (Latin for "to bless") was written as a 2005 new year's blessing honoring the 70th birthday of a friend (and his new titanium hip!) celebrated during a winter hike on the Appalachian Trail. The first stanza of this poem, which inspired the composition, is a traditional Irish blessing. The line "when hope and history rhyme" is taken from a Seamus Heaney poem entitled "On the far side of revenge."

Bread-baking God was originally written as a Mother's Day present for my mom. A slightly different version of this prayer was published in *Prayers for a Thousand Years: Inspiration from leaders and visionaries around the world*, Elizabeth Roberts and Elias Amidon, eds., HarperSanFrancisco 1999.

Come to the Waters. The evening's sermon was titled "The Common Purse and the God of Maximum Return."

For what do we hope? *As-salaam alaykum* and *Wa alaykum as-salaam* are phrases used, respectively, for the traditional greeting and response in Arabic.

Labor Day was written for a service marking the U.S. observance of Labor Day.

Only this is sure. Mount Mitchell, not far from Asheville, N.C., is the highest mountain east of the Mississippi River. Town Mountain runs through the city of Asheville.

Proclaim liberty was written for a service marking U.S. Independence Day.

Rizpah's vigil may be sung to the tune of "My Shepherd Will Supply My Need."

Satisfy the earth was written for an Earth Day celebration.

Send me. One of our nine-year-olds read the leader's part in this litany, which was earlier published in *Christian Feminism Today*, Summer 2008.

'Til earth receive her rest may be sung to the tune of "Amazing Grace."

Index of Scripture references

131 – No fright scars the night
145 – Heaven's delight and earth's repose
148 – Acclaim the One whose breath is your bounty
148:3, 7-10, 13 – Satisfy the earth

Isaiah
6:1-8 – Send me
21:8-9, 14-15 – Keeping Watch
33:7, 9, 10 – Satisfy the earth
40:4-5 – Satisfy the earth
55 – Come to the waters
55:12 – Satisfy the earth

Jeremiah
1:7-9 – Send me
31:31-34 – Heart religion

Lamentations
3 – Great is your faithfulness

Ezekiel
2:1-15 – Rouse yourselves
11:19-20 – Heart religion
34:1-14 – Pentecostal passion
34:11-22 – Come again and feed the earth

Hosea
2:18 – Satisfy the earth
4:1, 3 – Satisfy the earth

Amos
9:13 – Satisfy the earth

Habakkuk
1:1-4; 2:1-4 – Pound the doors of heaven
2:9-11 – Satisfy the earth

Matthew
2:16 – Annunciation

Acknowledgements

Much as I wish it otherwise, I rarely have the urge to write outside concrete circumstances—up to my eyeballs with particular people, wrangling with particular concerns, hanging on to outrageous hope against ponderous odds. So if there be any merit in this material, my own congregation, Circle of Mercy, shares the credit. The link between good speaking and good listening, between good writing and good reading, is more fluid—and more important—than most think.

Gratitude goes to several other individuals. Rev. Cindy Weber was the first to say "you need to share this stuff" after visiting our Circle, planting in my head the idea for this collection. Abigail Hastings, among my longest-standing friends (and an in-law), convinced me I should do this even though publishers insisted poetry doesn't sell. She then offered hours-upon-hours of a true poet's hand. Joyce Hollyday volunteered to pause work on her own new book to proofread. Dale Roberts, who heard much of this material read for the first time from worship bulletins, provided consistent encouragement long before the idea for this collection was hatched. Every worship planner deserves at least one Dale Roberts.

I once swore that if I ever did this—write an *acknowledgements* note for a book—I would never patronize my wife with a sentimental mention. But there's nothing sentimental about the accumulated decades of shared joy and laughter, grief and heartache, not to mention countless days ingloriously ruled by meal-prep and meetings and dubious achievements.

Nancy was not involved in writing this book, any more than I gave birth to our babies. But she was there through it all: the conception and gestation, the labor and delivery, inspiring and *conspiring.* —*KLS*

Order copies of *In the Land of the Living* through this website:

news ✣ commentary ✣ contemplation

An online journal
exploring the intersections of
personal, pastoral and prophetic faith

prayerandpolitiks.org

Ken Sehested, editor

About the author

Kenneth L. Sehested was born in Oklahoma and reared in West Texas and South Louisiana. A *cum laude* graduate of New York University, he received his Master of Divinity degree from Union Theological Seminary in New York City. He is married to Rev. Nancy Hastings Sehested, whose parish includes 800 inmates and 400 staff at a maximum security men's prison.

In 2001, along with Nancy and another colleague, Joyce Hollyday, he was the founding co-pastor of Circle of Mercy Congregation, affiliated with the Alliance of Baptists and the United Church of Christ, in Asheville, N.C. In 1984 he was the founding director of the Baptist Peace Fellowship of North America, a position he held for 18 years.

Sehested's writing includes four edited works (most recently, *Peace Primer: Quotes from Christian and Islamic Scripture and Tradition*, with Rabia Terry Harris, director of the Muslim Peace Fellowship), contributions to another dozen books (most recently, *Feasting on the Word: Preaching the Revised Common Lectionary*, David L. Bartlett and Barbara Brown Taylor, eds.) and articles in two dozen journals. His activism has taken him to more than 20 countries as a speaker, journalist and conflict mediator.